THE BASIC

DIANETICS

PICTURE BOOK

BASED ON THE WORKS OF

L. RON HUBBARD

Published in the United States by
Bridge Publications, Inc.
4751 Fountain Avenue
Los Angeles, California 90029

ISBN 0-88404-727-X

Published in other countries by
NEW ERA® Publications International ApS
Store Kongensgade 55
1264 Copenhagen K, Denmark

ISBN 87-7336-836-9

Printed in the United States of America

IMPORTANT NOTE

In reading this book, be very certain you never go past a word you do not fully understand.

The only reason a person gives up a study or becomes confused or unable to learn is because he or she has gone past a word that was not understood.

The confusion or inability to grasp or learn comes *after* a word that the person did not have defined and understood.

Have you ever had the experience of coming to the end of a page and realizing you didn't know what you had read? Well, somewhere earlier on that page you went past a word that you had no definition for or an incorrect definition for.

Here's an example. "It was found that when the crepuscule arrived the children were quieter and when it was not present, they were much livelier." You see what happens. You think you don't understand the whole idea, but the inability to understand came entirely from the one word you could not define, *crepuscule,* which means twilight or darkness.

It may not only be the new and unusual words that you will have to look up. Some commonly used words can often be misdefined and so cause confusion.

This datum about not going past an undefined word is the most important fact in the whole subject of study. Every subject you have taken up and abandoned had its words which you failed to get defined.

Therefore, in reading this book be very, very certain you never go past a word you do not fully understand. If the material becomes confusing or you can't seem to grasp it, there will be a word just earlier that you have not understood. Don't go any further, but go back to *before* you got into trouble, find the misunderstood word and get it defined.

DIANETICS

DIANETICS IS A TECHNOLOGY WHICH UNCOVERS THE SOURCE OF UNWANTED SENSATIONS AND EMOTIONS, ACCIDENTS, INJURIES AND PSYCHOSO-MATIC ILLNESSES, AND WHICH SETS FORTH EFFECTIVE HANDLINGS FOR THESE CONDITIONS.

DIANETICS WAS RESEARCHED AND DEVELOPED BY L. RON HUBBARD.

THIS BOOK PRESENTS THE BASIC DISCOVERIES OF DIANETICS AND THEIR APPLICATION IN RIDDING A PERSON OF THE BARRIERS WHICH KEEP HIM FROM BEING WELL AND HAPPY AND ACHIEVING HIS GOALS.

THE MIND AND YOUR SURVIVAL

DIANETICS IS AN EXPLORATION INTO THE HUMAN MIND, THAT VAST AND HITHERTO UNKNOWN REALM HALF AN INCH BACK OF OUR FOREHEADS.

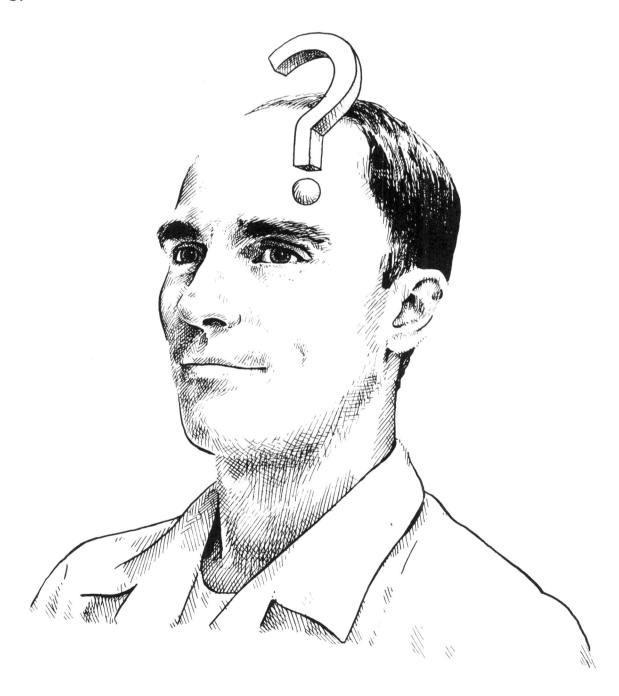

A SCIENCE OF MIND IS A GOAL WHICH HAS ENGROSSED THOUSANDS OF GENERATIONS OF MAN.

6

WHY DOES MAN SOMETIMES
BEHAVE IRRATIONALLY?

HOW CAN YOU OVERCOME THE BARRIERS THAT KEEP YOU FROM BEING HAPPY AND REACHING YOUR GOALS?

IN ORDER TO ANSWER THAT QUESTION, ONE MUST FIRST UNDERSTAND THE BASIC PURPOSES AND ACTIONS OF LIFE ITSELF.

THE GOAL OF LIFE CAN BE CONSIDERED TO BE INFINITE SURVIVAL. MAN, AS A LIFE FORM, CAN BE DEMONSTRATED TO OBEY IN ALL HIS ACTIONS AND PURPOSES THE ONE COMMAND: "SURVIVE!"

8

IT IS NOT A NEW THOUGHT THAT MAN IS SURVIVING. IT IS A NEW THOUGHT THAT MAN IS MOTIVATED *ONLY* BY SURVIVAL.

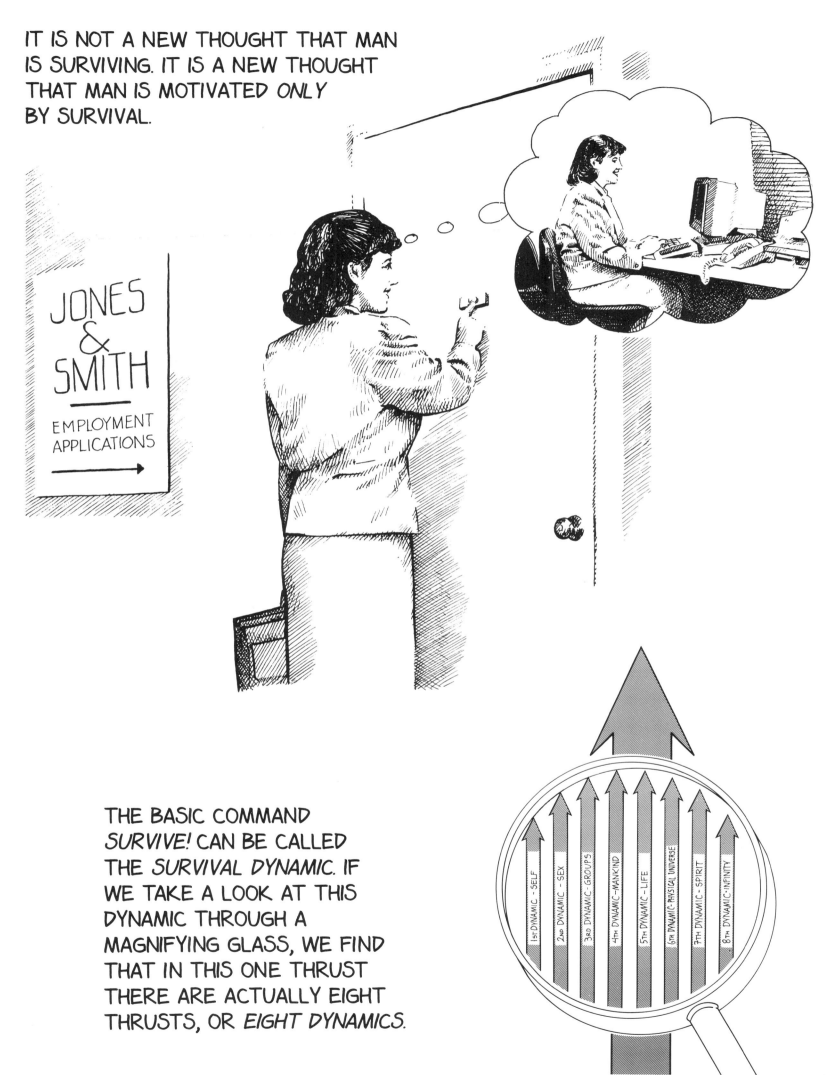

THE BASIC COMMAND *SURVIVE!* CAN BE CALLED THE *SURVIVAL DYNAMIC.* IF WE TAKE A LOOK AT THIS DYNAMIC THROUGH A MAGNIFYING GLASS, WE FIND THAT IN THIS ONE THRUST THERE ARE ACTUALLY EIGHT THRUSTS, OR *EIGHT DYNAMICS.*

I. THE DYNAMIC OF SELF

CONSISTS OF THE DYNAMIC THRUST TO
SURVIVE AS AN INDIVIDUAL, TO OBTAIN
PLEASURE AS AN INDIVIDUAL AND TO
AVOID PAIN. IT COVERS THE GENERAL
FIELD OF FOOD, CLOTHING AND SHELTER,
PERSONAL AMBITION AND GENERAL
INDIVIDUAL PURPOSE.

II. THE DYNAMIC OF SEX

EMBRACES THE PROCREATION
OF PROGENY (CHILDREN OR OFFSPRING),
THE CARE OF THAT PROGENY
AND THE SECURING FOR
THAT PROGENY OF
BETTER SURVIVAL
CONDITIONS AND
ABILITIES IN THE
FUTURE.

III. THE DYNAMIC OF GROUP

EMBRACES VARIOUS UNITS OF THE SPECIES OF MAN, SUCH
AS AN ASSOCIATION, A MILITARY COMPANY, THE PEOPLE IN
THE SURROUNDING COUNTRYSIDE, A NATION OR A RACE.
IT IS CHARACTERIZED BY ACTIVITY ON THE PART OF
THE INDIVIDUAL TO OBTAIN AND MAINTAIN
THE SURVIVAL
OF THE
GROUP OF
WHICH HE
IS A PART.

IV. THE MANKIND DYNAMIC

EMBRACES THE SURVIVAL OF
THE SPECIES.

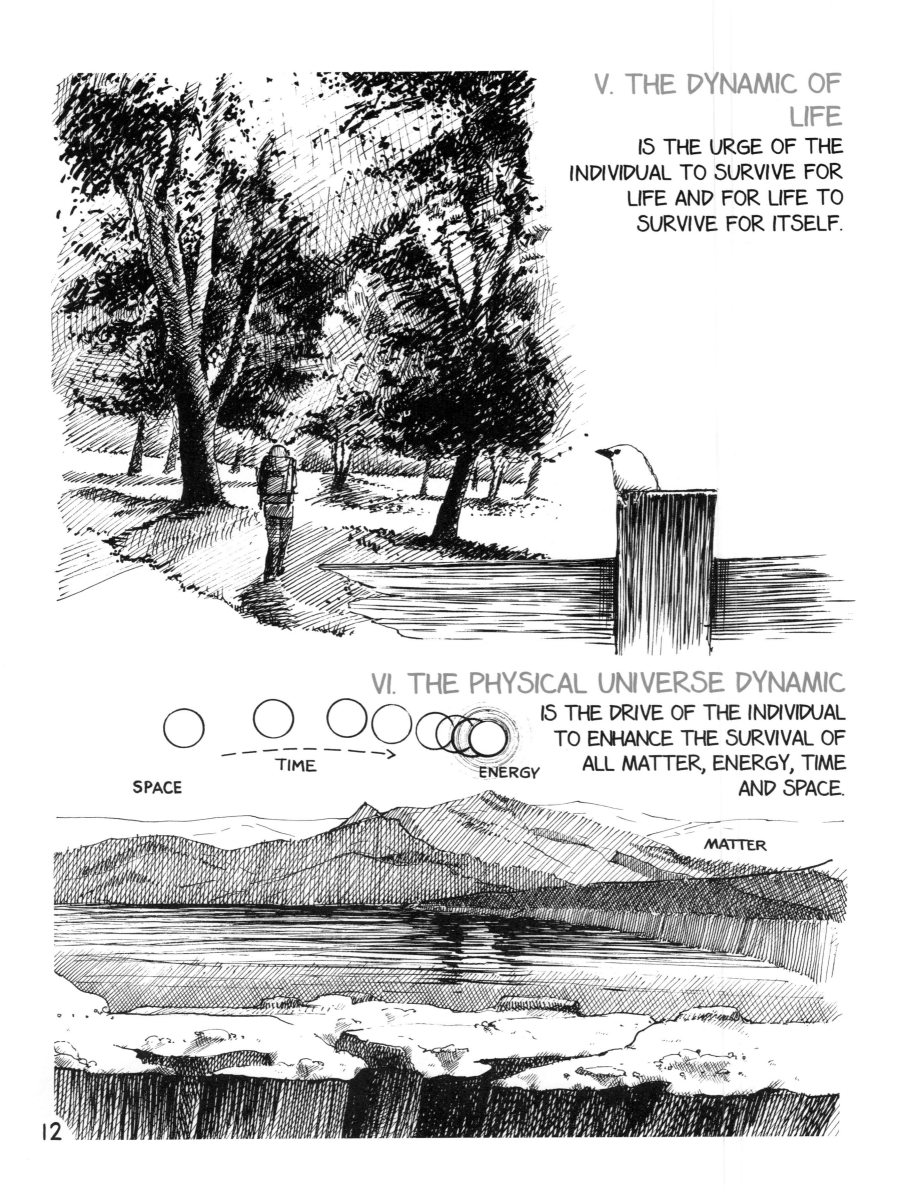

V. THE DYNAMIC OF LIFE

IS THE URGE OF THE INDIVIDUAL TO SURVIVE FOR LIFE AND FOR LIFE TO SURVIVE FOR ITSELF.

VI. THE PHYSICAL UNIVERSE DYNAMIC

IS THE DRIVE OF THE INDIVIDUAL TO ENHANCE THE SURVIVAL OF ALL MATTER, ENERGY, TIME AND SPACE.

SPACE

TIME

ENERGY

MATTER

VII. THE SPIRITUAL DYNAMIC

IS THE URGE TOWARD EXISTENCE AS OR OF SPIRITS.

VIII. THE INFINITY DYNAMIC

IS THE URGE TOWARD EXISTENCE AS INFINITY. THIS IS ALSO IDENTIFIED AS THE SUPREME BEING. THIS IS CALLED THE EIGHTH DYNAMIC BECAUSE THE SYMBOL OF INFINITY STOOD UPRIGHT MAKES THE NUMERAL 8.

THE THRUST OF SURVIVAL IS TOWARD PLEASURE AND AWAY FROM PAIN. BY *PLEASURE* IS MEANT "GRATIFICATION; AGREEABLE EMOTIONS, MENTAL OR PHYSICAL; TRANSIENT ENJOYMENT; OPPOSED TO PAIN."

BY *PAIN* IS MEANT "PHYSICAL OR MENTAL SUFFERING; PENALTY."

THE REWARD OF SURVIVAL
ACTIVITY IS *PLEASURE.*

THE ULTIMATE PENALTY OF DESTRUCTIVE
ACTIVITY IS DEATH OR COMPLETE
NONSURVIVAL, AND IS *PAIN.*

THE PURPOSE OF THE MIND IS TO SOLVE
PROBLEMS RELATING TO SURVIVAL.

THE MIND DIRECTS THE INDIVIDUAL IN THE EFFORT OF SURVIVAL ACROSS THE EIGHT DYNAMICS. IT OPERATES BASED UPON THE INFORMATION THAT IT RECEIVES OR RECORDS.

THAT A PERSON FAILS OR MAKES A MISTAKE DOES NOT ALTER THE FACT THAT HIS BASIC MOTIVATION WAS SURVIVAL.

THUS, THE MIND AS THE CENTRAL DIRECTION SYSTEM OF THE BODY, POSES, PERCEIVES AND RESOLVES PROBLEMS OF SURVIVAL . . .

. . . AND DIRECTS OR FAILS TO DIRECT THEIR EXECUTION.

19

FAILURES LOWER THE SURVIVAL
POTENTIAL TOWARD DEATH.

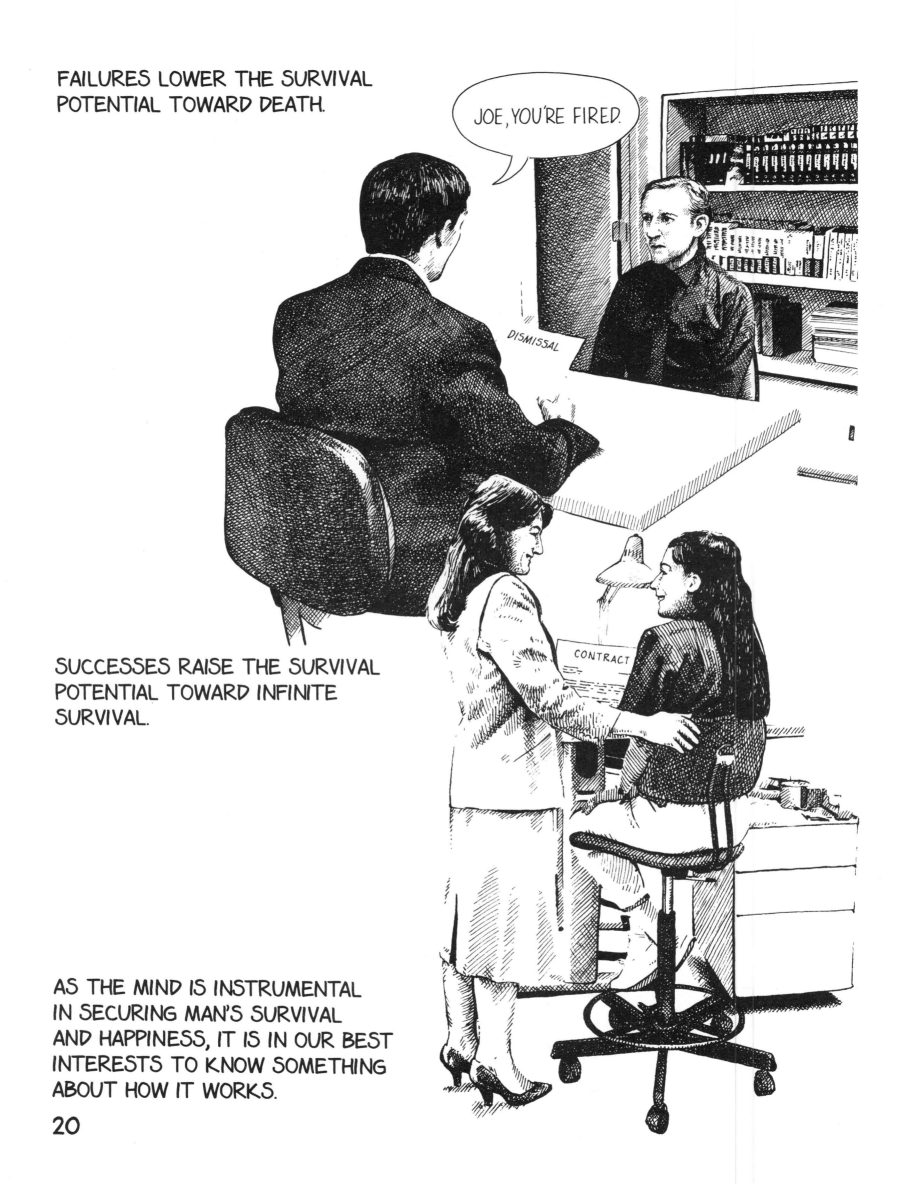

SUCCESSES RAISE THE SURVIVAL
POTENTIAL TOWARD INFINITE
SURVIVAL.

AS THE MIND IS INSTRUMENTAL
IN SECURING MAN'S SURVIVAL
AND HAPPINESS, IT IS IN OUR BEST
INTERESTS TO KNOW SOMETHING
ABOUT HOW IT WORKS.

THE PARTS OF THE MIND

THE HUMAN MIND CAN BE CONSIDERED TO HAVE TWO MAJOR DIVISIONS.

THE ANALYTICAL MIND

THE FIRST OF THESE TWO PARTS IS THE *ANALYTICAL MIND*. THIS IS THE CONSCIOUS, AWARE MIND WHICH THINKS, OBSERVES DATA, REMEMBERS IT AND RESOLVES PROBLEMS.

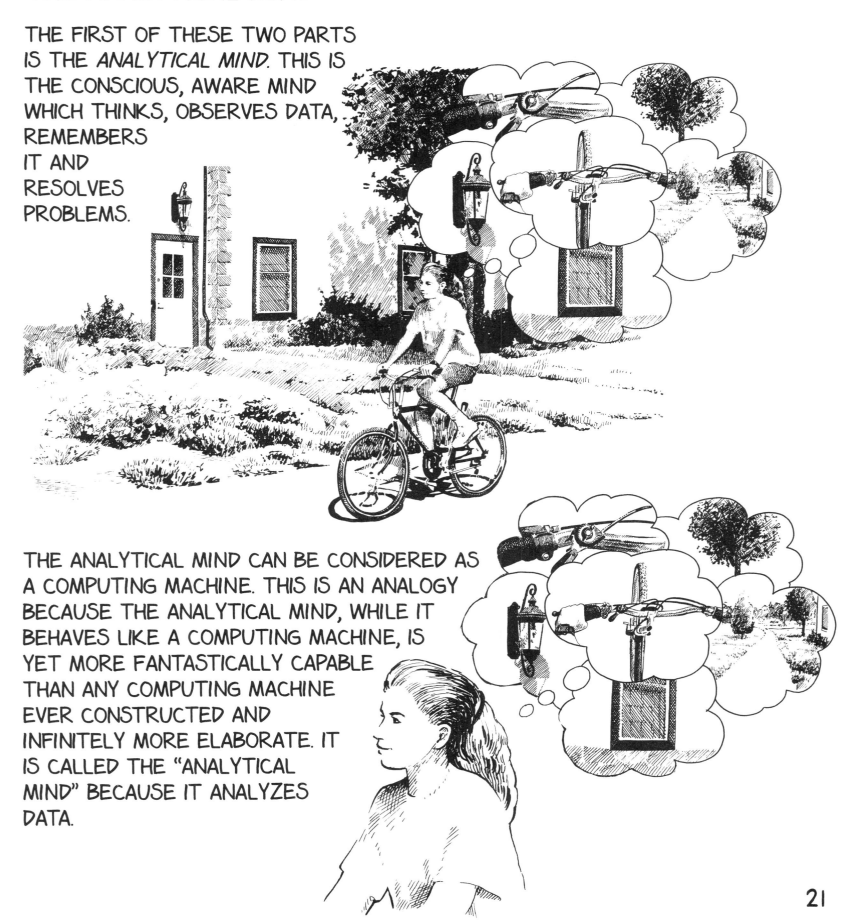

THE ANALYTICAL MIND CAN BE CONSIDERED AS A COMPUTING MACHINE. THIS IS AN ANALOGY BECAUSE THE ANALYTICAL MIND, WHILE IT BEHAVES LIKE A COMPUTING MACHINE, IS YET MORE FANTASTICALLY CAPABLE THAN ANY COMPUTING MACHINE EVER CONSTRUCTED AND INFINITELY MORE ELABORATE. IT IS CALLED THE "ANALYTICAL MIND" BECAUSE IT ANALYZES DATA.

THE ANALYTICAL MIND THINKS IN *DIFFERENCES* AND *SIMILARITIES.*

IT IS NOT JUST A *GOOD* COMPUTER, IT IS A *PERFECT* COMPUTER. IT NEVER MAKES A MISTAKE. IT CANNOT ERR IN ANY WAY SO LONG AS A HUMAN BEING IS REASONABLY INTACT (UNLESS SOMETHING HAS CARRIED AWAY A PIECE OF HIS MENTAL EQUIPMENT).

MENTAL IMAGE PICTURES

THE ANALYTICAL MIND HAS ITS STANDARD MEMORY BANKS. THE DATA IN THESE MEMORY BANKS IS FILED IN RECORDINGS CALLED *MENTAL IMAGE PICTURES.*

HERE'S A DEMONSTRATION YOU CAN DO: CLOSE YOUR EYES AND THINK OF A CAT FOR A FEW SECONDS.

DID YOU GET A PICTURE OF A CAT? IT DOESN'T MATTER IF THE PICTURE WAS CLEAR OR JUST A HAZY IMPRESSION.

THAT IS A MENTAL IMAGE PICTURE.

MENTAL IMAGE PICTURES ARE THREE-DIMENSIONAL COLOR PICTURES WITH SOUND AND SMELL AND ALL OTHER PERCEPTIONS, PLUS THE CONCLUSIONS OR SPECULATIONS OF THE INDIVIDUAL.

THESE PICTURES ARE ACTUALLY COMPOSED OF ENERGY. THEY HAVE MASS, THEY EXIST IN SPACE AND THEY FOLLOW SOME VERY, VERY DEFINITE ROUTINES OF BEHAVIOR, THE MOST INTERESTING OF WHICH IS THE FACT THAT THEY APPEAR WHEN SOMEBODY THINKS OF SOME-THING. HE THINKS OF A CERTAIN DOG, HE GETS A PICTURE OF THE DOG.

THE
TIME
TRACK

PAST

THE MIND CONTAINS A CONSECU-TIVE RECORD OF MENTAL IMAGE PICTURES WHICH ACCUMULATES THROUGH THE PRECLEAR'S LIFE. THIS IS CALLED THE *TIME TRACK*. IT IS VERY EXACTLY DATED.

24

THE TIME TRACK IS A VERY ACCURATE
RECORD OF THE PRECLEAR'S PAST, VERY
ACCURATELY TIMED. IF MOTION PICTURE
FILM WERE THREE-DIMENSIONAL, HAD
FIFTY-TWO PERCEPTIONS AND COULD
FULLY REACT UPON THE OBSERVER,
THE TIME TRACK COULD BE CALLED
A MOTION PICTURE FILM.

IT IS THE ENTIRE SEQUENCE
OF "NOW" INCIDENTS,
COMPLETE WITH ALL SENSE
MESSAGES, PICKED UP BY A
PERSON DURING HIS LIFE.

PRESENT

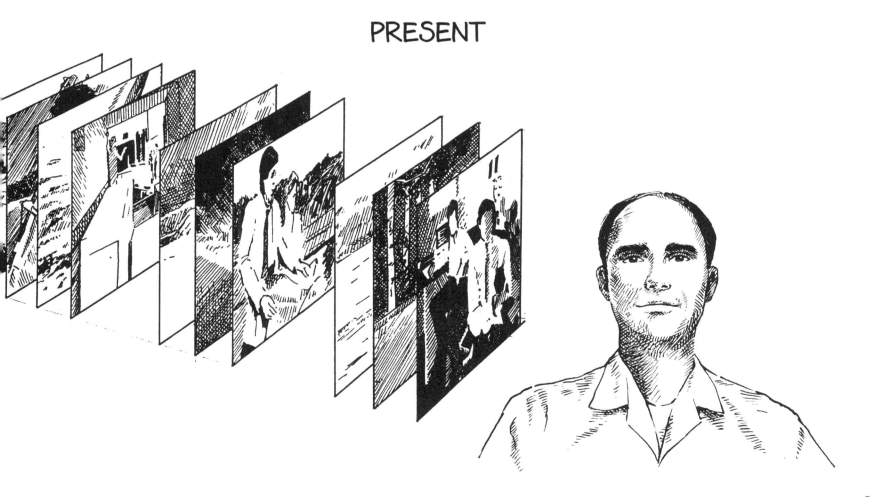

THE ANALYTICAL MIND USES THE DATA IN THE
STANDARD MEMORY BANKS TO MAKE
DECISIONS THAT WILL PROMOTE
SURVIVAL.

SAVE OUR
FORESTS

THIS IS SANITY. THIS IS
HAPPINESS. THIS IS
SURVIVAL.
WHERE IS THE ERROR?

THE REACTIVE MIND

THERE ARE TWO THINGS WHICH APPEAR TO BE—BUT ARE NOT—RECORDED IN THE STANDARD BANKS: PAINFUL EMOTION AND PHYSICAL PAIN. IN MOMENTS OF INTENSE PAIN, THE ACTION OF THE ANALYTICAL MIND IS SUSPENDED, AND THE SECOND PART OF THE MIND, THE *REACTIVE MIND,* TAKES OVER.

ANALYTICAL MIND

REACTIVE MIND

WHEN A PERSON IS FULLY CONSCIOUS, HIS ANALYTICAL MIND IS FULLY IN COMMAND OF THE ORGANISM. WHEN THE INDIVIDUAL IS "UNCONSCIOUS" IN FULL OR IN PART, THE REACTIVE MIND IS CUT IN, IN FULL OR IN PART.

THE SHOCK OF ACCIDENTS, THE ANESTHETICS USED FOR OPERATIONS, THE PAIN OF INJURIES AND THE DELIRIUMS OF ILLNESS ARE THE PRINCIPAL SOURCES OF WHAT WE CALL "UNCONSCIOUSNESS."

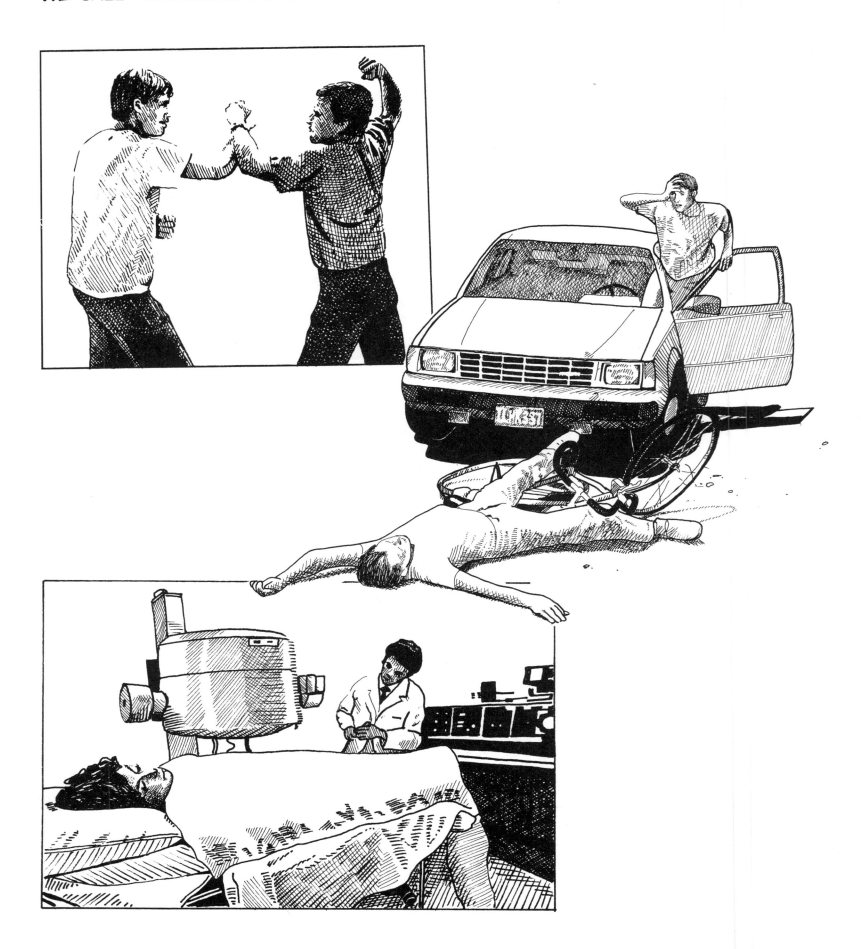

THE REACTIVE MIND CONTINUES TO MAKE PICTURES
NO MATTER HOW "UNCONSCIOUS" A PERSON
SUPPOSEDLY IS.

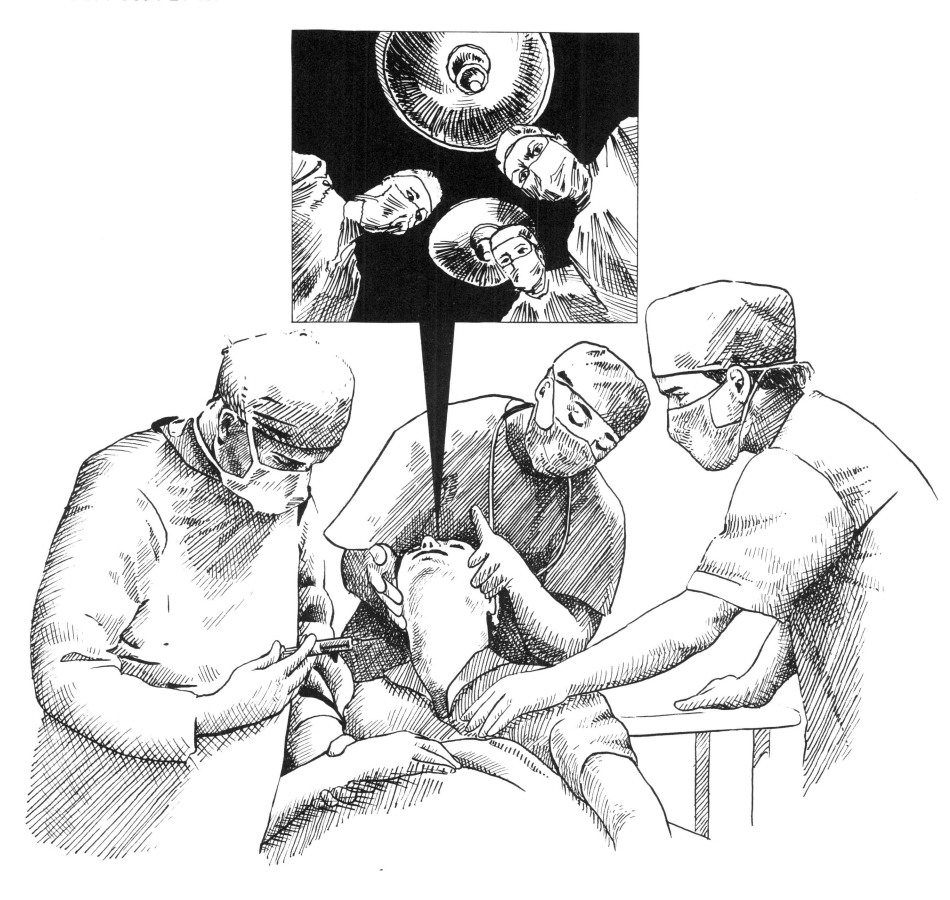

THE REACTIVE MIND WORKS ON A TOTALLY
STIMULUS-RESPONSE BASIS (GIVEN A CERTAIN
STIMULUS, IT GIVES A CERTAIN RESPONSE). IT
IS NOT UNDER THE INDIVIDUAL'S VOLITIONAL
CONTROL, AND IT EXERTS FORCE AND THE
POWER OF COMMAND OVER HIS AWARENESS,
PURPOSES, THOUGHTS, BODY AND ACTIONS.

IT IS THIS MIND WHICH STORES UP PICTURES
OF ALL THE BAD OR PAINFUL THINGS THAT
HAVE HAPPENED TO ONE . . .

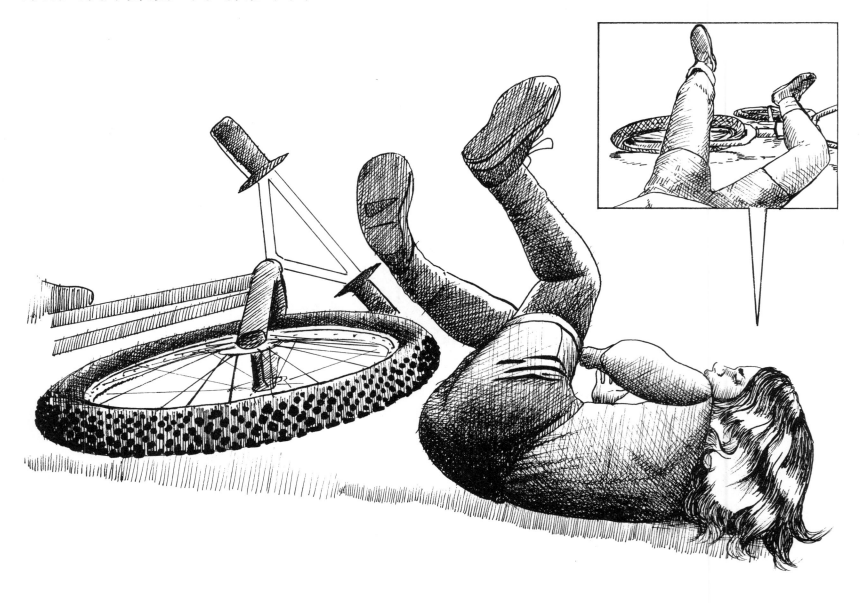

. . . AND THROWS THEM BACK TO HIM AGAIN IN MOMENTS OF EMERGENCY OR DANGER SO AS TO DICTATE HIS ACTIONS ALONG LINES WHICH HAVE BEEN CONSIDERED "SAFE" BEFORE. THIS IS CALLED *RESTIMULATION.*

THE REACTIVE MIND DOES NOT STORE MEMORIES AS WE KNOW THEM. IT STORES *ENGRAMS*. THESE ENGRAMS ARE A COMPLETE RECORDING, DOWN TO THE LAST ACCURATE DETAIL, OF EVERY PERCEPTION PRESENT IN A MOMENT OF PARTIAL OR FULL "UNCONSCIOUSNESS."

THIS IS AN EXAMPLE OF AN ENGRAM: A WOMAN IS KNOCKED DOWN BY A BLOW. SHE IS RENDERED "UNCONSCIOUS." SHE IS KICKED AND TOLD SHE IS A FAKER, THAT SHE IS NO GOOD, THAT SHE IS ALWAYS CHANGING HER MIND. A CHAIR IS OVERTURNED IN THE PROCESS. A FAUCET IS RUNNING IN THE KITCHEN. A CAR IS PASSING IN THE STREET OUTSIDE. THE ENGRAM CONTAINS A RUNNING RECORD OF ALL THESE PERCEPTIONS.

THE PROBLEM WITH THE REACTIVE MIND IS THAT IT "THINKS" IN *IDENTITIES*, ONE THING *IDENTICAL* TO ANOTHER. THE EQUATION IS A = A = A = A = A. A REACTIVE MIND COMPUTATION ABOUT THIS ENGRAM WOULD BE: THE PAIN OF THE KICK *EQUALS* THE PAIN OF THE BLOW *EQUALS* THE OVERTURNING CHAIR *EQUALS* THE PASSING CAR *EQUALS* THE FAUCET *EQUALS* THE FACT THAT SHE IS A FAKER *EQUALS* THE FACT THAT SHE IS NO GOOD *EQUALS* THE FACT THAT SHE CHANGES HER MIND *EQUALS* THE VOICE TONES OF THE MAN *EQUALS* THE EMOTION *EQUALS* A FAKER *EQUALS* A FAUCET RUNNING *EQUALS* THE PAIN OF THE KICK *EQUALS* ORGANIC SENSATION IN THE AREA OF THE KICK *EQUALS* THE OVER-TURNING CHAIR *EQUALS* CHANGING ONE'S MIND *EQUALS* . . . BUT WHY CONTINUE? EVERY SINGLE PERCEPTION IN THIS ENGRAM *EQUALS* EVERY OTHER PERCEPTION IN THIS ENGRAM.

FAKER

ANY PERCEPTION IN THE ENGRAM RECEIVED HAS SOME QUALITY OF RESTIMULATION. WHEN THIS WOMAN'S PRESENT ENVIRONMENT CONTAINS ENOUGH SIMILARITIES TO THE ELEMENTS FOUND IN THE ENGRAM, SHE WILL EXPERIENCE A REACTIVATION OF THE ENGRAM. THE MECHANISM IS TELLING HER THAT SHE IS IN DANGEROUS QUARTERS. IF SHE STAYS, THE PAINS IN THE AREAS WHERE SHE WAS ABUSED CAN BECOME A PREDISPOSITION TO ILLNESS OR A CHRONIC ILLNESS IN THEMSELVES.

THE WORDS IN THE ENGRAM ARE ALSO TAKEN LITERALLY AND USED AS COMMANDS BY THE REACTIVE MIND. WHEN THE ENGRAM IS RESTIMULATED IN ONE OF THE GREAT MANY WAYS POSSIBLE, SHE HAS A "FEELING" THAT SHE IS NO GOOD, A FAKER, AND SHE WILL CHANGE HER MIND.

34

HERE IS AN EXAMPLE OF HOW THE
REACTIVE MIND WORKS:

A GIRL GETS BITTEN BY A DOG.

GET AWAY FROM THAT MAD DOG!

SHE RETAINS A PICTURE OF
THIS EXPERIENCE IN THE
REACTIVE MIND—AN ENGRAM.

GET AWAY FROM THAT MAD DOG!

YEARS LATER, AT A POINT WHEN SHE IS SOMEWHAT TIRED OR SLIGHTLY SICK AND HER ANALYTICAL MIND ISN'T AT TOP CAPACITY, SHE PASSES A DOG ON THE STREET . . .

. . . AND ENOUGH OF THE ELEMENTS ARE SIMILAR TO THE ORIGINAL ENGRAM TO RESTIMULATE IT. THE REACTIVE MIND BECOMES ACTIVE TO "PROTECT" THE GIRL FROM WHAT IT CONCEIVES TO BE A DANGEROUS SITUATION.

THE ENGRAM IS *BELOW* THE GIRL'S CONSCIOUS AWARENESS. SHE MAY NOT EVEN REALIZE THAT SHE HAS SEEN A DOG . . . .

. . . BUT HER ARM BEGINS TO HURT AND SHE FEELS THAT SHE HAS TO GET AWAY. SHE DOES NOT KNOW WHY.

I BETTER RUSH HOME. IT SCARES ME TO LEAVE BABY JOE WITH A BABYSITTER ALL DAY LONG. BESIDES, THIS HEAVY SHOPPING BAG IS STARTING TO HURT MY ARM.

GET AWAY FROM THAT MAD DOG!

AND ANOTHER EXAMPLE:

A PERSON HAS AN ACCIDENT WHILE SWIMMING AND ALMOST DROWNS.

YEARS LATER, A RESTIMULATION OF THE ENGRAM CAN CAUSE HIM TO HAVE TROUBLE BREATHING.

THE REACTIVE MIND IS VERY RUGGED, BUT IT IS NOT VERY REFINED. ALTHOUGH ITS PURPOSE IS TO AID THE INDIVIDUAL'S SURVIVAL BY HELPING HIM TO AVOID SITUATIONS WHICH HAVE PROVEN HARMFUL IN THE PAST . . .

. . . IN ACTUAL FACT THE COURSES OF
ACTION DICTATED BY THE REACTIVE MIND
ARE OFTEN NOT SAFE, BUT HIGHLY
DANGEROUS.

THE REACTIVE MIND
COMPRISES AN
UNKNOWING, UNWANTED
SERIES OF ABERRATED
COMPUTATIONS WHICH
BRING ABOUT AN EFFECT
UPON THE INDIVIDUAL
AND THOSE AROUND HIM.

THE MECHANICS OF THE REACTIVE MIND

THERE ARE THREE SPECIFIC TYPES OF MENTAL IMAGE PICTURES IN THE REACTIVE MIND.

ENGRAM

AS COVERED EARLIER, THE MOST BASIC OF THESE IS THE *ENGRAM*. AN ENGRAM IS A MENTAL IMAGE PICTURE WHICH IS A RECORDING OF A TIME OF PHYSICAL PAIN AND UNCONSCIOUSNESS. IT MUST BY DEFINITION HAVE IMPACT OR INJURY AS PART OF ITS CONTENT.

41

AN ENGRAM CONTAINS EVERY PERCEPTION PRESENT IN A MOMENT OF PARTIAL OR FULL UNCONSCIOUSNESS.

SECONDARY

A *SECONDARY* IS A MENTAL IMAGE PICTURE OF A MOMENT OF SEVERE AND SHOCKING LOSS OR THREAT OF LOSS WHICH CONTAINS MISEMOTION (AN EMOTION OR EMOTIONAL REACTION THAT IS INAPPROPRIATE TO THE PRESENT TIME SITUATION) SUCH AS ANGER, FEAR, GRIEF, APATHY OR "DEATHFULNESS." IT IS A MENTAL IMAGE RECORDING OF A TIME OF SEVERE MENTAL STRESS. IT MAY CONTAIN UNCONSCIOUSNESS.

A SECONDARY IS CALLED A SECONDARY BECAUSE IT ITSELF DEPENDS UPON AN EARLIER ENGRAM WITH SIMILAR DATA BUT REAL PAIN.

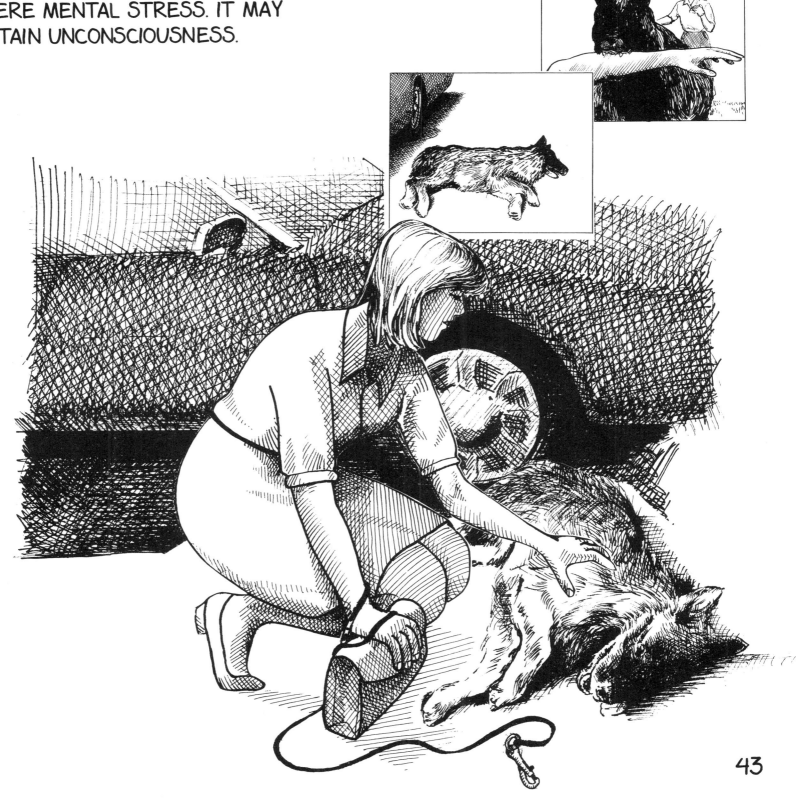

GET AWAY FROM THAT MAD DOG!

LOCK

A *LOCK* IS A MENTAL IMAGE PICTURE OF AN EXPERIENCE WHERE ONE WAS KNOWINGLY OR UNKNOWINGLY REMINDED OF A SECONDARY OR ENGRAM.

IT DOES NOT ITSELF CONTAIN A BLOW OR A BURN OR IMPACT AND IS NOT ANY MAJOR CAUSE OF MISEMOTION. IT DOES NOT CONTAIN UNCON-SCIOUSNESS. IT MAY CONTAIN A FEELING OF PAIN OR ILLNESS, ETC., BUT IS NOT ITSELF THE SOURCE OF IT.

INCIDENT

AN *INCIDENT* IS THE RECORDING OF AN EXPERIENCE, SIMPLE OR COMPLEX, RELATED BY THE SAME SUBJECT, LOCATION OR PEOPLE, UNDERSTOOD TO TAKE PLACE IN A SHORT AND FINITE TIME PERIOD SUCH AS MINUTES OR HOURS OR DAYS.

AN INCIDENT CAN BE AN ENGRAM, SECONDARY, KEY-IN (A MOMENT WHEN THE ENGRAM IS RESTIMULATED) OR LOCK.

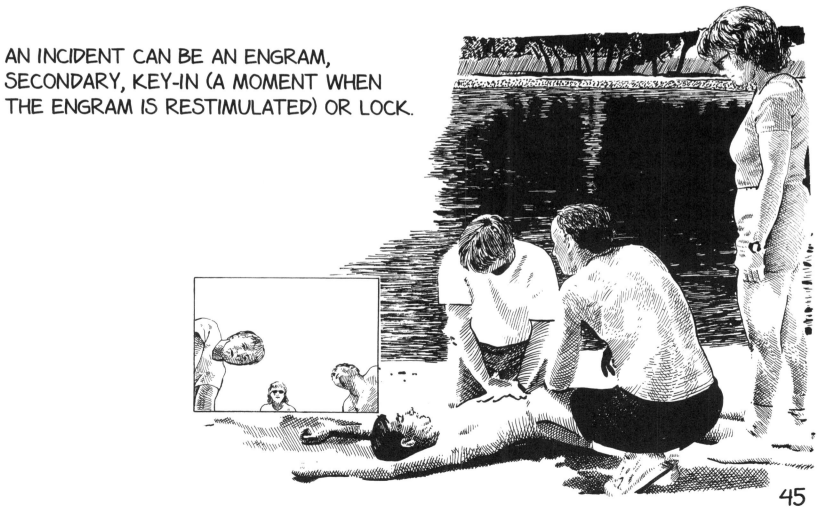

CHAIN

ENGRAMS, SECONDARIES AND LOCKS FORM INTO CHAINS. A *CHAIN* IS A SERIES OF RECORDINGS OF SIMILAR EXPERIENCES. A CHAIN HAS ENGRAMS, SECONDARIES AND LOCKS. THE ENGRAM IS THE EARLIEST DATE, THE SECONDARY A LATER DATE, THE LOCK THE MOST RECENT.

HERE IS AN EXAMPLE OF A CHAIN. THE FIRST EXPERIENCE IS AN *ENGRAM*.

ONCE THE PERSON HAS AN ENGRAM ON A SUBJECT, A SUBSEQUENT EXPERIENCE WHICH INCLUDES A MOMENT OF SEVERE LOSS OR THREAT OF LOSS CAN BE RECORDED AS A *SECONDARY* ON THE CHAIN. IT GETS ITS FORCE AND IS HELD IN PLACE BY THE EARLIER ENGRAM.

LATER, WHEN THE PERSON SEES SOMETHING THAT REMINDS HIM, KNOWINGLY OR UNKNOWINGLY, OF THE ENGRAM, HE CAN GET A *LOCK* ADDED TO THE CHAIN.

THIS LEAVES THE PERSON WITH A CHAIN OF THREE PICTURES—A LOCK, A SECONDARY AND AN ENGRAM, THE CHAIN BEING HELD IN PLACE BY THE ENGRAM WHICH IS THE BASIC (EARLIEST) PICTURE.

47

EACH TIME THE CHAIN KEYS IN (IS RESTIMULATED OR REACTIVATED) A NEW LOCK IS FORMED ON IT.

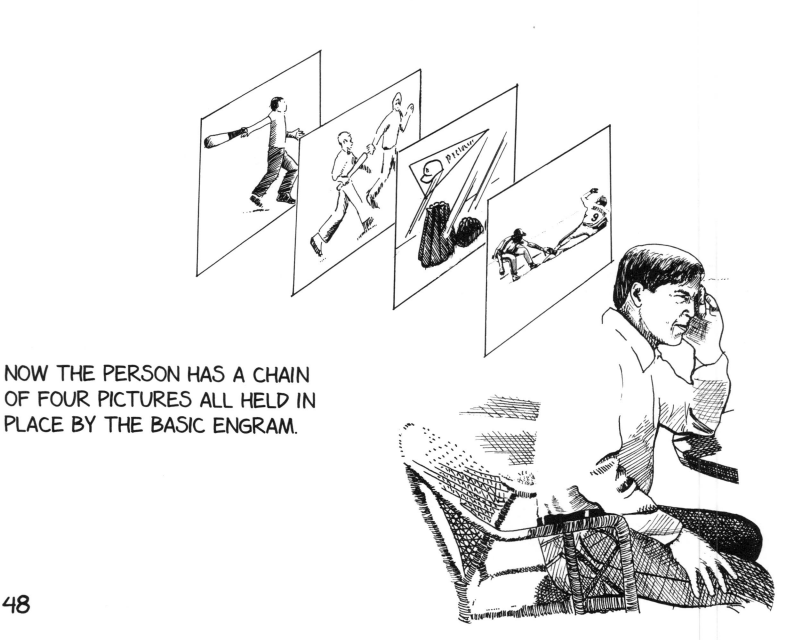

NOW THE PERSON HAS A CHAIN OF FOUR PICTURES ALL HELD IN PLACE BY THE BASIC ENGRAM.

ANOTHER HEAD INJURY CONTAINING PAIN AND UNCONSCIOUSNESS WOULD ADD A NEW ENGRAM TO THE CHAIN.

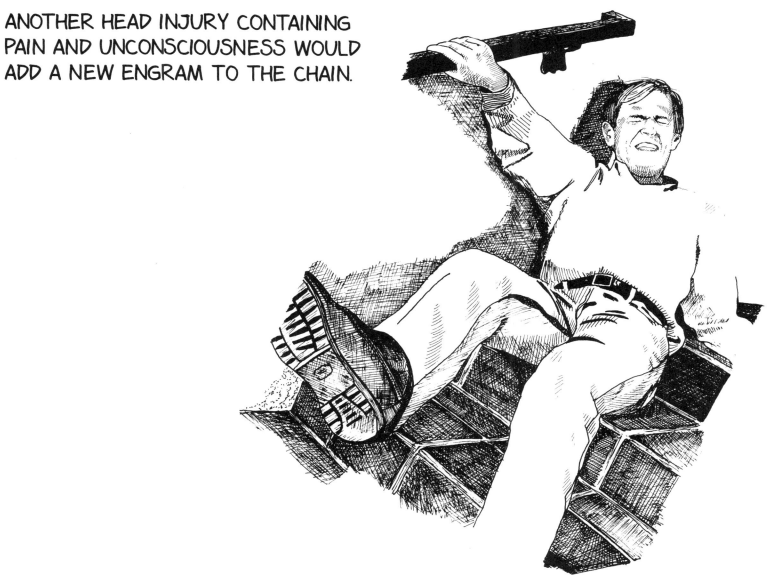

THIS NOW LEAVES THE PERSON WITH A CHAIN OF FIVE PICTURES ALL HELD IN PLACE BY THE BASIC ENGRAM ON THE CHAIN.

MORE SECONDARIES, LOCKS AND
ENGRAMS CAN ACCUMULATE ON
THE CHAIN.

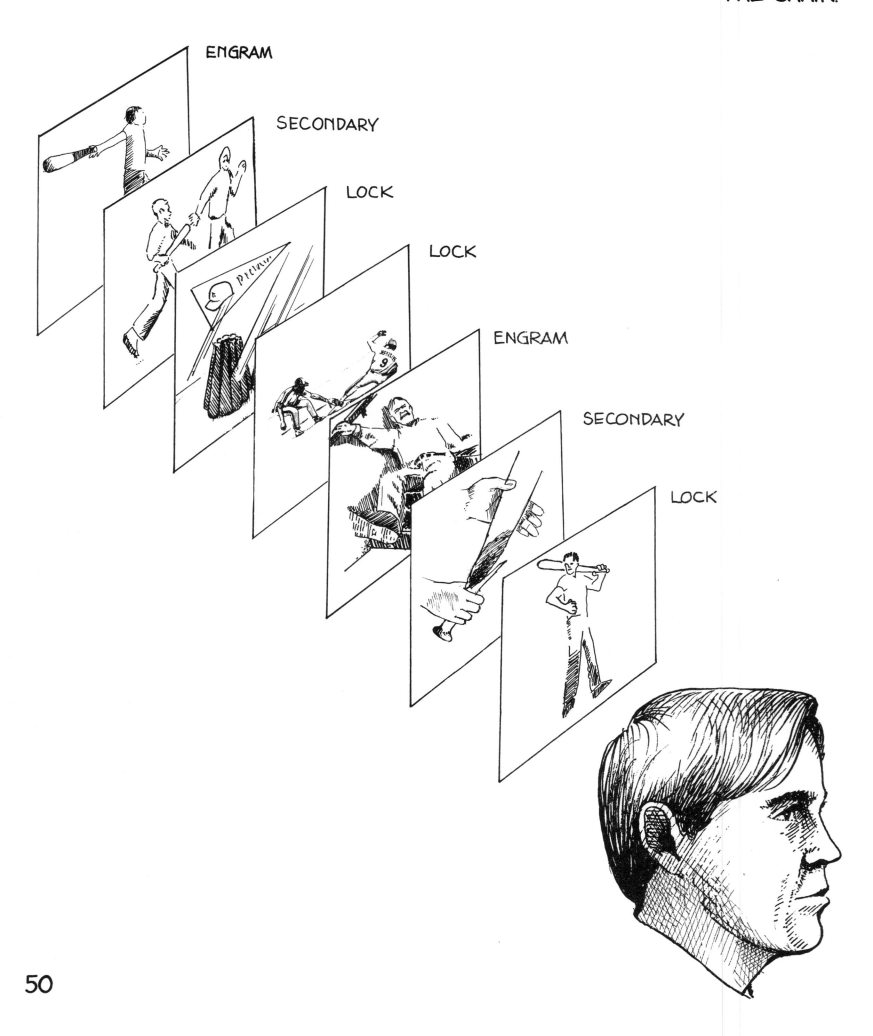

50

AND A PERSON CAN HAVE
MANY, MANY CHAINS OF THIS KIND, EACH ONE
BEING HELD IN PLACE BY A BASIC ENGRAM.

MENTAL MASS

THERE IS MASS CONTAINED IN THE MENTAL
IMAGE PICTURES IN THE REACTIVE MIND,
CALLED *MENTAL MASS*. THESE PICTURES
HAVE ACTUAL WEIGHT; VERY TINY, BUT
THEY HAVE WEIGHT, AND THEY ACTUALLY
HAVE SIZE AND SHAPE. THEIR PROPOR-
TIONATE WEIGHT WOULD BE TERRIBLY
SLIGHT COMPARED TO THE REAL
OBJECT WHICH THE PERSON IS
MAKING A PICTURE OF.

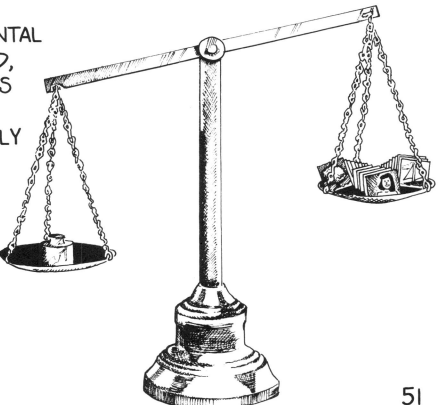

CHARGE

CHARGE IS THE STORED QUANTITIES OF ENERGY IN THE TIME TRACK. IT IS HARMFUL ENERGY OR FORCE ACCUMULATED AND STORED WITHIN THE REACTIVE MIND, RESULTING FROM THE

CONFLICTS AND UNPLEASANT EXPERIENCES THAT A PERSON HAS HAD.

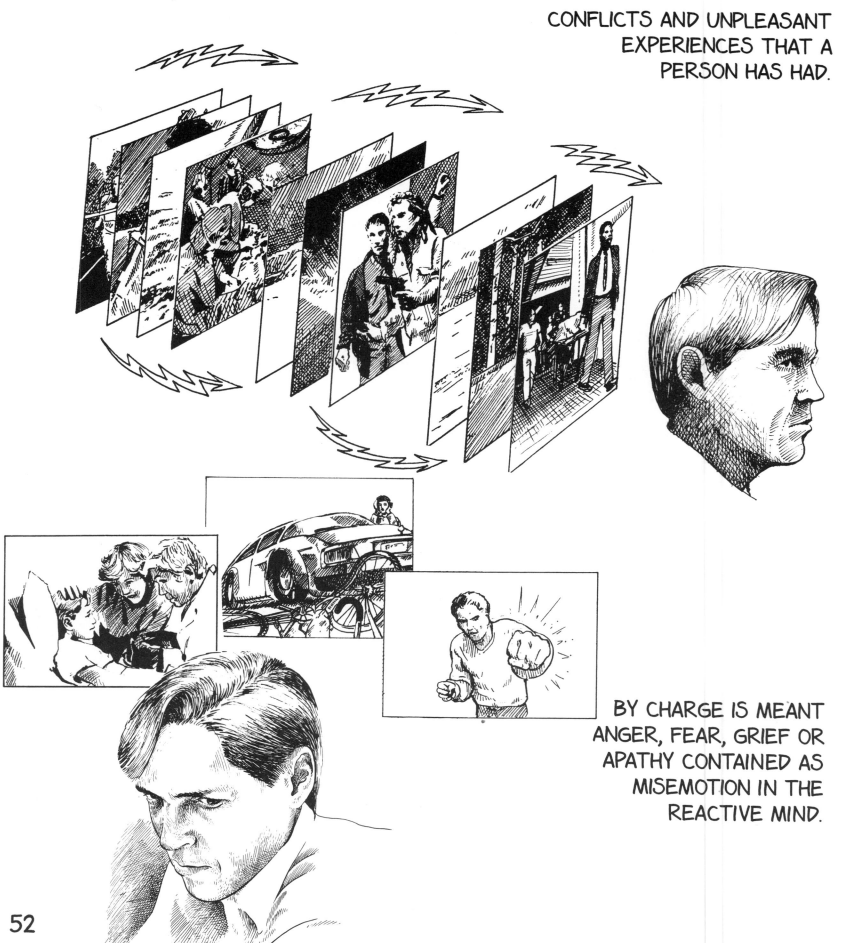

BY CHARGE IS MEANT ANGER, FEAR, GRIEF OR APATHY CONTAINED AS MISEMOTION IN THE REACTIVE MIND.

ENGRAMS, SECONDARIES, LOCKS, ALL ADD
UP TO MENTAL MASSES, FORCES, ENERGIES,
TIME, WHICH EXPRESS THEMSELVES IN
COUNTLESS DIFFERENT WAYS . . .

. . . SUCH AS PAIN, FEELINGS, OLD PERCEPTIONS, INAPPROPRIATE EMOTIONAL REACTIONS AND A BILLION BILLION THOUGHT COMBINATIONS BURIED IN THE MASSES AS SIGNIFICANCES.

BOY, I THINK WHAT I SAID TO JOANNE JUST NOW WAS REALLY <u>STUPID</u>. I MUST BE AN <u>IDIOT</u>. AND THE SIDE OF MY HEAD IS REALLY STARTING TO ACHE.

YOU STUPID IDIOT!

THE GOAL OF DIANETICS

DIANETICS CONTAINS TECHNIQUES WHICH CAN RID A PERSON OF THE ADVERSE EFFECTS OF ENGRAMS, SECONDARIES AND LOCKS. THE APPLICATION OF DIANETICS TECHNIQUES TO SOMEONE IS CALLED *AUDITING*.

DIANETICS CAN BE APPLIED BY ANY TWO PEOPLE ON A MUTUAL AUDITING BASIS USING THE FIRST BOOK WRITTEN ON THE SUBJECT, *DIANETICS: THE MODERN SCIENCE OF MENTAL HEALTH.* THIS TECHNIQUE, EXACTLY AS USED IN THE 1950s, IS STILL TAUGHT TODAY IN SEMINARS AROUND THE WORLD. IN JUST A FEW HOURS, ANYONE CAN LEARN TO AUDIT DIANETICS.

MANY ADVANCES AND REFINEMENTS WERE MADE IN DIANETICS TECHNOLOGY IN LATER YEARS, LEADING TO THE RELEASE IN

1978 OF *NEW ERA DIANETICS*—A GREATLY STREAMLINED AUDITING PROCEDURE THAT GETS FASTER AND BETTER RESULTS. NEW ERA DIANETICS IS ONLY AUDITED BY A FULLY TRAINED PRACTITIONER.

ANALYTICAL MIND

REACTIVE MIND

THE GOAL OF DIANETICS IS THE *CLEAR*. A CLEAR IS A BEING WHO NO LONGER HAS HIS OWN REACTIVE MIND.

THE CLEAR HAS NO ENGRAMS WHICH CAN BE RESTIMULATED TO THROW OUT THE CORRECTNESS OF COMPUTATION BY ENTERING HIDDEN AND FALSE DATA. THE CLEAR'S MIND BRINGS FORTH ANSWERS WHICH ARE INVARIABLY ACCURATE, THE SOLUTIONS MODIFIED ONLY BY OBSERVATION, EDUCATION AND VIEWPOINT.

THE DRIVE STRENGTH OF THE PERSON DOES
NOT DERIVE FROM HIS ABERRATIONS. THE
ABERRATIONS LESSEN THE DRIVE
STRENGTH.

ARTISTRY, PERSONAL FORCE, PERSONALITY,
ARE ALL RESIDUAL IN THE BASIC PERSON-
ALITY OF THE PERSON, NOT THE REACTIVE
MIND.

BECOMING CLEAR STRENGTHENS A
PERSON'S NATIVE INDIVIDUALITY AND
CREATIVITY RATHER THAN IN ANY WAY
DIMINISHING THESE.

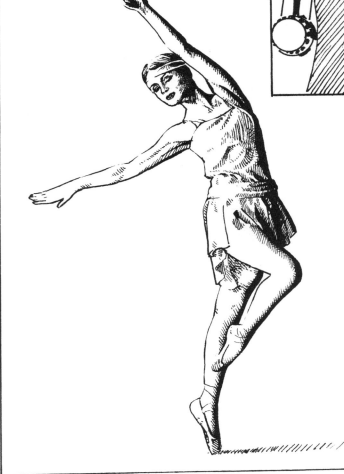

THE STATE OF CLEAR
IS ATTAINED THROUGH
DIANETICS AUDITING.

NEW ERA DIANETICS AUDITING

THE EXACT DEFINITION OF *AUDITING* IS: THE ACTION OF ASKING A PERSON A QUESTION (WHICH HE CAN UNDERSTAND AND ANSWER), GETTING AN ANSWER TO THAT QUESTION AND ACKNOWLEDGING HIM FOR THAT ANSWER.

A PERSON WHO IS RECEIVING DIANETICS AUDITING AND IS THEREFORE ON THE ROAD TO BECOMING CLEAR IS CALLED A *PRECLEAR*.

A PERSON TRAINED AND QUALIFIED IN APPLYING DIANETICS PROCEDURES TO INDIVIDUALS FOR THEIR BETTERMENT IS CALLED AN AUDITOR. *AUDITOR MEANS ONE WHO LISTENS.*

RETURNING

THERE IS AN INHERENT, NOT TAUGHT, ABILITY OF THE REMEMBERING MECHANISMS OF THE MIND WHICH IS USED IN DIANETICS AUDITING. THIS ABILITY IS TERMED *RETURNING*. WHAT THIS MEANS IS THAT THE PERSON CAN "SEND" A PORTION OF HIS MIND TO A PAST PERIOD ON EITHER A MENTAL OR COMBINED MENTAL AND PHYSICAL BASIS AND CAN REEXPERIENCE INCIDENTS WHICH HAVE TAKEN PLACE IN HIS PAST IN THE SAME FASHION AND WITH THE SAME SENSATIONS AS BEFORE.

A PERSON CAN, FOR EXAMPLE, GO BACK TO A TIME WHEN HE WAS SWIMMING AND SWIM WITH FULL RECALL OF HEARING, SIGHT, TASTE, SMELL, ORGANIC SENSATION, TACTILE, ETC.

THE WATER IS VERY COLD, AND I CAN SMELL THE CHLORINE IN THE POOL...

THIS IS NOT DONE USING HYPNOSIS, DRUGS OR TRANCE TECHNIQUES. PART OF THE MIND CAN "RETURN" EVEN WHEN A PERSON IS WIDE-AWAKE AND REEXPERIENCE PAST INCIDENTS IN FULL.

THE E-METER

THE AUDITOR TRAINED IN NEW ERA DIANETICS ALSO USES A HIGH-TECH ELECTRONIC DEVICE TO HELP FIND THE CHARGED AREAS ON THE PRECLEAR'S TIME TRACK. THIS DEVICE IS CALLED AN *ELECTROPSYCHOMETER,* OR *E-METER.* THE E-METER MEASURES THE MENTAL STATE OR CHANGE OF STATE OF A PERSON.

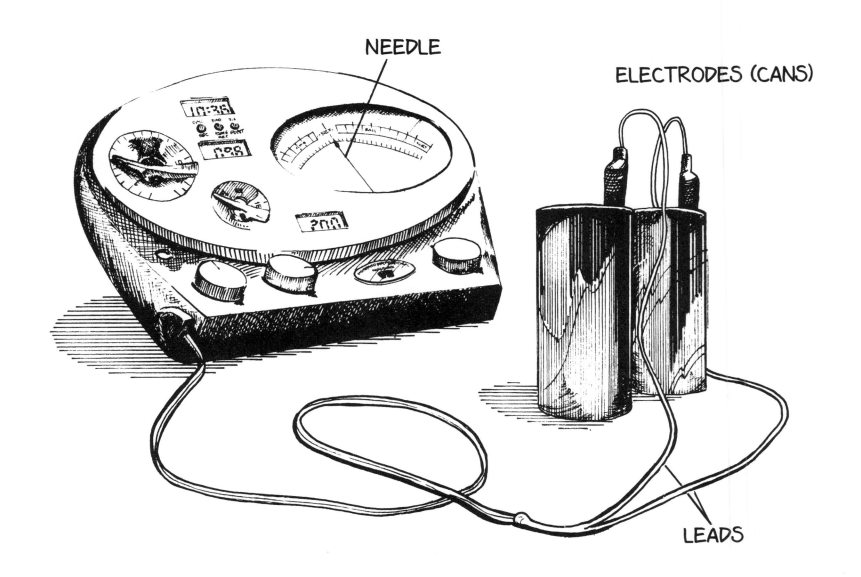

NEEDLE

ELECTRODES (CANS)

LEADS

THE E-METER IS A RELIGIOUS ARTIFACT AND CAN ONLY BE USED BY AUDITORS WHO ARE MINISTERS OR MINISTERS IN TRAINING. IT DOES NOT DIAGNOSE OR CURE ANYTHING. IT IS USED BY THE AUDITOR TO HELP LOCATE SPECIFICALLY WHAT SHOULD BE ADDRESSED IN AUDITING.

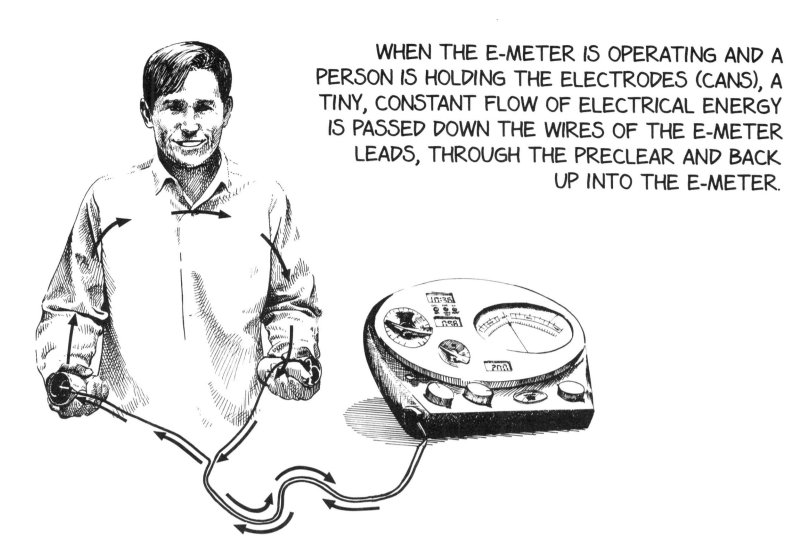

WHEN THE E-METER IS OPERATING AND A PERSON IS HOLDING THE ELECTRODES (CANS), A TINY, CONSTANT FLOW OF ELECTRICAL ENERGY IS PASSED DOWN THE WIRES OF THE E-METER LEADS, THROUGH THE PRECLEAR AND BACK UP INTO THE E-METER.

WHEN THE PRECLEAR THINKS A THOUGHT, LOOKS AT A PICTURE, REEXPERIENCES AN INCIDENT OR SHIFTS SOME PART OF THE REACTIVE MIND, HE IS MOVING AND CHANGING ACTUAL MENTAL MASS AND ENERGY.

65

THESE CHANGES IN THE PRECLEAR'S MIND INFLUENCE THE TINY FLOW OF ELECTRICAL ENERGY GENERATED BY THE E-METER, CAUSING THE NEEDLE TO MOVE. THE NEEDLE REACTIONS ON THE E-METER TELL THE AUDITOR WHERE THE CHARGE LIES AND WHAT TO HANDLE.

NEW ERA DIANETICS AUDITING HAS A SET PROCEDURE CONSISTING OF CERTAIN QUESTIONS AND COMMANDS WHICH THE AUDITOR GIVES THE PRECLEAR.

THE PRECLEAR IS ASKED BY THE AUDITOR TO "RETURN" TO AN INCIDENT FROM HIS PAST CONTAINING PAIN OR UNPLEASANT EMOTION.

HE IS ASKED TO RECOUNT EXACTLY WHAT OCCURRED IN THAT INCIDENT, FROM BEGINNING TO END.

IF, WHILE RECOUNTING THE INCIDENT, IT SEEMS TO BE GOING MORE SOLID RATHER THAN LESSENING . . .

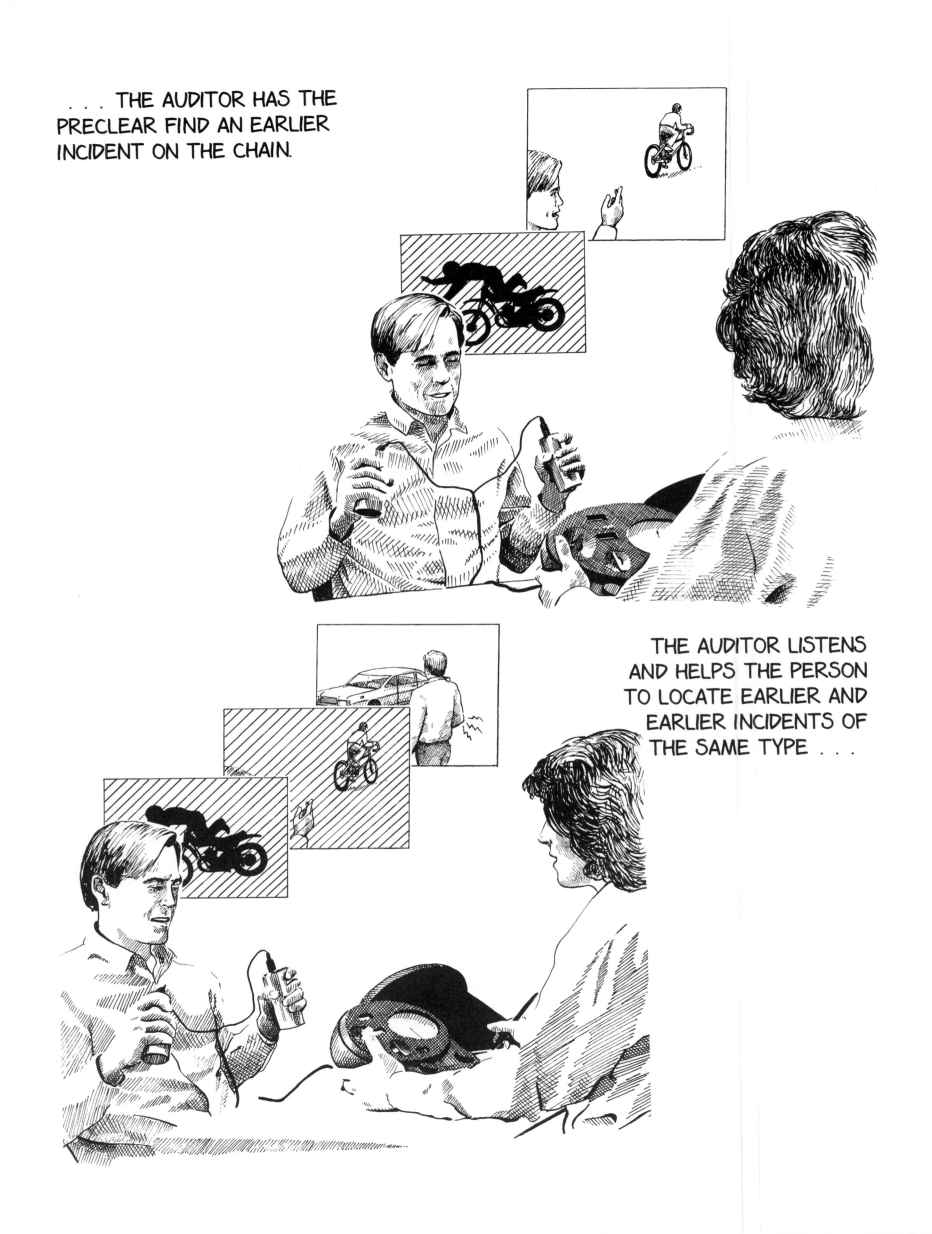

. . . THE AUDITOR HAS THE PRECLEAR FIND AN EARLIER INCIDENT ON THE CHAIN.

THE AUDITOR LISTENS AND HELPS THE PERSON TO LOCATE EARLIER AND EARLIER INCIDENTS OF THE SAME TYPE . . . .

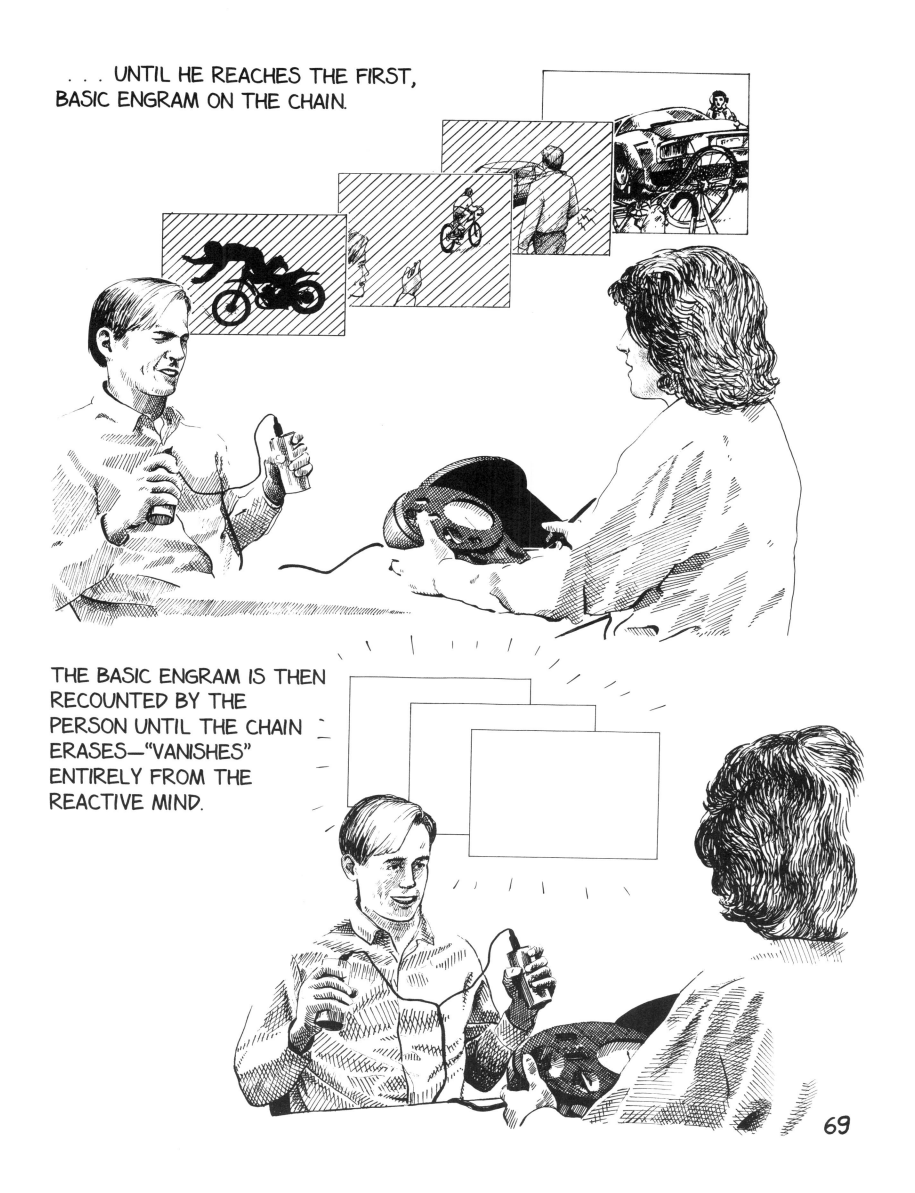

... UNTIL HE REACHES THE FIRST, BASIC ENGRAM ON THE CHAIN.

THE BASIC ENGRAM IS THEN RECOUNTED BY THE PERSON UNTIL THE CHAIN ERASES—"VANISHES" ENTIRELY FROM THE REACTIVE MIND.

ERASURE IS THE ACTION OF ERASING, RUBBING OUT, LOCKS, SECONDARIES OR ENGRAMS. IT IS THE APPARENT REMOVAL OF THE INCIDENT FROM THE FILES OF THE REACTIVE MIND AND REFILING OF IT AS EXPERIENCE IN THE ANALYTICAL MIND.

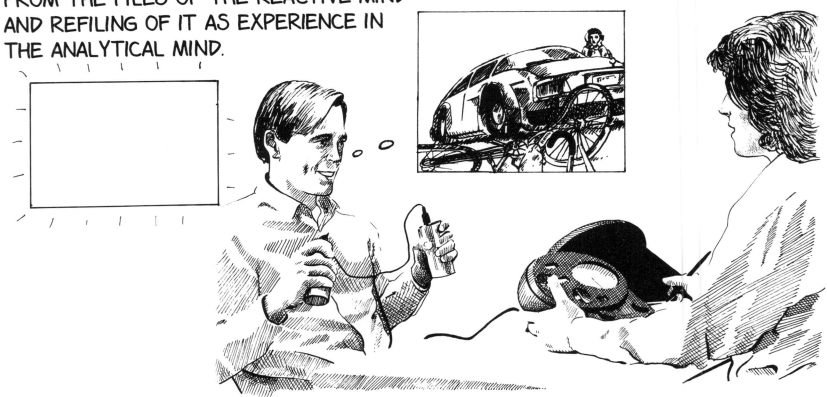

AS EACH CHAIN IS TRACED BACK AND ERASED THROUGH DIANETICS AUDITING, THE ADVERSE EFFECTS OF THE REACTIVE MIND ARE LESSENED AND THE INDIVIDUAL BECOMES HAPPIER AND MORE IN CONTROL OF HIS LIFE.

THE END RESULT IS A CLEAR—A PERSON WHO NO LONGER HAS HIS OWN REACTIVE MIND.

FREED OF THE REACTIVE MIND, A PERSON CAN BE HAPPIER, MORE SELF-CONFIDENT, MORE EFFECTIVE AND SUCCESSFUL IN HIS ENDEAVORS.

DIANETICS IS AN ADVENTURE.

TREAT IT AS AN ADVENTURE.

AND MAY YOU NEVER BE THE SAME AGAIN.

FIND OUT MORE ABOUT DIANETICS.

For more information about Dianetics and
books by L. Ron Hubbard

Call: *1-800-367-8788*

or contact any of the organizations
listed in the back of this book.

*Call this toll-free number 7 days a week
from 9 A.M. to 11 P.M. Pacific Standard Time.*

ABOUT THE AUTHOR

L. Ron Hubbard is one of the most acclaimed and widely read authors of all time, primarily because his works express a firsthand knowledge of the nature of man—knowledge gained not from standing on the sidelines but through lifelong experience with people from all walks of life.

As Ron said, "One doesn't learn about life by sitting in an ivory tower, thinking about it. One learns about life by being part of it." And that is how he lived.

He began his quest for knowledge on the nature of man at a very early age. When he was eight years old he was already well on his way to being a seasoned traveler. His adventures included voyages to China, Japan and other points in the Orient and South Pacific, covering a quarter of a million miles by the age of nineteen. In the course of his travels he became closely acquainted with twenty-one different races and cultures all over the world.

In the fall of 1930, Ron pursued his studies of mathematics and engineering, enrolling at George Washington University where he was also a member of one of the first American classes on nuclear physics. He realized that neither the East nor the West contained the full answer to the problems of existence. Despite all of mankind's advances in the physical sciences, a *workable* technology of the mind and life had never been developed. The mental "technologies" which did exist, psychology and psychiatry, were actually barbaric, false subjects—no more workable than the methods of jungle witch doctors. Ron shouldered the responsibility of filling this gap in the knowledge of mankind.

He financed his early research through fiction writing. He became one of the most highly demanded authors in the golden age of popular adventure and science fiction writing during the 1930s and 1940s, interrupted only by his service in the US Navy during World War II.

Partially disabled at the war's end, Ron applied what he had learned from his researches. He made breakthroughs and developed techniques which made it possible for him to recover from his injuries and help others to regain their health. It was during this time that the basic tenets of Dianetics technology were codified.

In late 1947, he wrote a manuscript detailing his discoveries. It was not published at that time, but circulated amongst Ron's friends, who copied it and passed it on to others. (This manuscript was formally published in 1951 as *Dianetics: The Original Thesis* and later republished as *The Dynamics of Life*.) The interest generated by this manuscript prompted a flood of requests for more information on the subject.

Ron provided all his discoveries to the American Psychiatric Association and the American Medical Association. Despite the fact that his work would have benefited them and society immensely, they ignored his research and continued on with their archaic activities.

Meanwhile, the steadily increasing flow of letters asking for further information and requesting that he detail more applications of his new subject resulted in Ron spending all his time answering letters. He decided to write and publish a comprehensive text on the subject— *Dianetics: The Modern Science of Mental Health.*

With the release of *Dianetics* on 9 May 1950, a complete handbook for the application of Ron's new technology was broadly available for the first time. Public interest spread like wildfire. The book shot to the top of the *New York Times* bestseller list and remained there week after week. More than 750 Dianetics study groups sprang up within a few months of its publication.

Ron's work did not stop with the success of *Dianetics* but accelerated, with new discoveries and breakthroughs a constant, normal occurrence. Throughout the 1950s, he continued to make further advances in the areas of the mind and the spirit.

In the early 1960s, Ron made startling breakthroughs in Dianetics procedure which resulted in dramatically increased speed of delivery, brought about unparalleled gains for preclears and formed the basis of today's modern engram-running procedure. Modern procedure, New Era Dianetics, was developed and released in 1978—the culmination of three decades of research into the effects of the spirit upon the body. With the advent of New Era Dianetics, preclears could locate and erase engrams with far greater precision and speed than ever before.

Through the 1960s, 70s and into the 80s, he continued his research and writing, amassing an enormous volume of material totaling over 60 million words—recorded in books, manuscripts and taped lectures. Today these works are studied and applied daily in hundreds of Dianetics centers and Scientology churches, missions and organizations around the world.

With his research fully completed and codified, L. Ron Hubbard departed his body on 24 January 1986.

Ron's work opened a wide bridge to understanding and freedom for mankind. Through his efforts, there now exists a totally workable technology with which people can help each other improve their lives and succeed in achieving their goals.

GET YOUR FREE CATALOG OF KNOWLEDGE ON HOW TO IMPROVE LIFE

L. Ron Hubbard's books and tapes increase your ability to understand yourself and others. His works give you the practical know-how you need to improve your life and the lives of your family and friends.

WRITE FOR YOUR FREE CATALOG TODAY!

Bridge Publications, Inc.
4751 Fountain Avenue
Los Angeles, California 90029

NEW ERA Publications International, ApS
Store Kongensgade 55
1264 Copenhagen K, Denmark

"I AM ALWAYS HAPPY TO HEAR FROM MY READERS."

L. RON HUBBARD

These were the words of L. Ron Hubbard, who was always very interested in hearing from his friends and readers. He made a point of staying in communication with everyone he came in contact with over his fifty-year career as a professional writer, and he had thousands of fans and friends that he corresponded with all over the world.

The publishers of L. Ron Hubbard's works wish to continue this tradition and welcome letters and comments from you, his readers, both old and new.

Additionally, the publishers will be happy to send you information on anything you would like to know about Ron, his extraordinary life and accomplishments and the vast number of books he has written.

Any message addressed to the Author's Affairs Director at Bridge Publications will be given prompt and full attention.

Bridge Publications, Inc.
4751 Fountain Avenue
Los Angeles, California 90029
USA

ADDRESS LIST

United States of America

Albuquerque
Hubbard Dianetics Foundation
8106 Menaul Blvd. NE
Albuquerque, New Mexico 87110

Ann Arbor
Hubbard Dianetics Foundation
122 S. Main, Suite 160
Ann Arbor, Michigan 48106

Atlanta
Hubbard Dianetics Foundation
2632 Piedmont Rd., NE
Atlanta, Georgia 30324

Austin
Hubbard Dianetics Foundation
2200 Guadalupe
Austin, Texas 78705

Boston
Hubbard Dianetics Foundation
448 Beacon Street
Boston, Massachusetts 02115

Buffalo
Hubbard Dianetics Foundation
47 West Huron Street
Buffalo, New York 14202

Chicago
Hubbard Dianetics Foundation
3011 North Lincoln Avenue
Chicago, Illinois 60657

Cincinnati
Hubbard Dianetics Foundation
215 West 4th Street, 5th Floor
Cincinnati, Ohio 45202

Clearwater
Hubbard Dianetics Foundation
Flag® Service Organization
210 South Fort Harrison Avenue
Clearwater, Florida 34616

Columbus
Hubbard Dianetics Foundation
167 East State Street
Columbus, Ohio 43215

Dallas
Hubbard Dianetics Foundation
Celebrity Centre® Dallas
8501 Manderville Lane
Dallas, Texas 75231

Denver
Hubbard Dianetics Foundation
375 South Navajo Street
Denver, Colorado 80223

Detroit
Hubbard Dianetics Foundation
321 Williams Street
Royal Oak, Michigan 48067

Honolulu
Hubbard Dianetics Foundation
1 N. King St., Lower Level
Honolulu, Hawaii 96817

Kansas City
Hubbard Dianetics Foundation
3619 Broadway
Kansas City, Missouri 64111

Las Vegas
Hubbard Dianetics Foundation
846 East Sahara Avenue
Las Vegas, Nevada 89104

Hubbard Dianetics Foundation
Celebrity Centre Las Vegas
1100 South 10th Street
Las Vegas, Nevada 89104

Long Island
Hubbard Dianetics Foundation
330 Fulton Avenue
Hempstead, New York 11550

Los Angeles and vicinity
Hubbard Dianetics Foundation
4810 Sunset Boulevard
Los Angeles, California 90027

Hubbard Dianetics Foundation
1451 Irvine Boulevard
Tustin, California 92680

Hubbard Dianetics Foundation
263 East Colorado Boulevard
Pasadena, California 91101

Hubbard Dianetics Foundation
10335 Magnolia Boulevard
North Hollywood, California 91601

Hubbard Dianetics Foundation
Celebrity Centre® International
5930 Franklin Avenue
Hollywood, California 90028

Miami
Hubbard Dianetics Foundation
120 Giralda Avenue
Coral Gables, Florida 33134

Minneapolis
Hubbard Dianetics Foundation
1011 Nicollet Mall
Minneapolis, Minnesota 55403

Mountain View
Hubbard Dianetics Foundation
2483 Old Middlefield Way
Mountain View, California 94043

New Haven
Hubbard Dianetics Foundation
909 Whalley Avenue
New Haven, Connecticut 06515

New York City
Hubbard Dianetics Foundation
227 West 46th Street
New York City, New York 10036

Hubbard Dianetics Foundation
Celebrity Centre New York
65 East 82nd Street
New York City, New York 10028

Orlando
Hubbard Dianetics Foundation
710-A East Colonial Drive
Orlando, Florida 32803

Philadelphia
Hubbard Dianetics Foundation
1315 Race Street
Philadelphia, Pennsylvania 19107

Phoenix
Hubbard Dianetics Foundation
4450 North Central Avenue, Suite 102
Phoenix, Arizona 85012

Portland
Hubbard Dianetics Foundation
323 SW Washington
Portland, Oregon 97204

Hubbard Dianetics Foundation
Celebrity Centre Portland
709 South West Salmon Street
Portland, Oregon 97205

Sacramento
Hubbard Dianetics Foundation
825 15th Street
Sacramento, California 95814

Salt Lake City
Hubbard Dianetics Foundation
1931 S. 1100 East
Salt Lake City, Utah 84106

San Diego
Hubbard Dianetics Foundation
701 "C" Street
San Diego, California 92101

San Francisco
Hubbard Dianetics Foundation
83 McAllister Street
San Francisco, California 94102

San Jose
Hubbard Dianetics Foundation
80 East Rosemary
San Jose, California 95112

Santa Barbara
Hubbard Dianetics Foundation
524 State Street
Santa Barbara, California 93101

Seattle
Hubbard Dianetics Foundation
2603 3rd Street
Seattle, Washington 98121

St. Louis
Hubbard Dianetics Foundation
9510 Page Boulevard
St. Louis, Missouri 63132

Tampa
Hubbard Dianetics Foundation
4809 North Armenia Avenue
Suite 215
Tampa, Florida 33603

Washington, DC
Hubbard Dianetics Foundation
2125 "S" Street NW
Washington, DC 20008

Canada

Edmonton
Hubbard Dianetics Foundation
10349 82nd Avenue
Edmonton, Alberta
Canada T6E 1Z9

Kitchener
Hubbard Dianetics Foundation
30 King St. East
Kitchener, Ontario
Canada N2G 2K6

Montréal
Centre de Dianétique Hubbard
4489 Papineau Street
Montréal, Québec
Canada H2H 1T7

Ottawa
Hubbard Dianetics Foundation
150 Rideau Street, 2nd Floor
Ottawa, Ontario
Canada K1N 5X6

Québec
Centre de Dianétique Hubbard
350 BD Charest Est
Québec, Québec
Canada G1K 3H5

Toronto
Hubbard Dianetics Foundation
696 Yonge Street
Toronto, Ontario
Canada M4Y 2A7

Vancouver
Hubbard Dianetics Foundation
405 West Hastings Street
Vancouver, British Columbia
Canada V6B 1L5

Winnipeg
Hubbard Dianetics Foundation
Suite 125–388 Donald Street
Winnipeg, Manitoba
Canada R3B 2J4

United Kingdom

Birmingham
Hubbard Dianetics Foundation
60/62 Constitution Hill
Birmingham
England B19 3JT

Brighton
Hubbard Dianetics Foundation
Dukes Arcade, Top Floor
Dukes Street
Brighton, Sussex
England BN1 1AG

East Grinstead
Hubbard Dianetics Foundation
Saint Hill Manor
East Grinstead, West Sussex
England RH19 4JY

Edinburgh
Hubbard Dianetics Foundation
20 Southbridge
Edinburgh, Scotland EH1 1LL

London
Hubbard Dianetics Foundation
68 Tottenham Court Road
London, England W1P 0BB

Manchester
Hubbard Dianetics Foundation
258 Deansgate
Manchester, England M3 4BG

Plymouth
Hubbard Dianetics Foundation
41 Ebrington Street
Plymouth, Devon
England PL4 9AA

Sunderland
Hubbard Dianetics Foundation
51 Fawcett Street
Sunderland, Tyne and Wear
England SR1 1RS

Austria

Vienna
Hubbard Dianetics Foundation
Schottenfeldgasse 13–15
1070 Vienna, Austria

Hubbard Dianetics Foundation
Celebrity Centre Vienna
Senefeldergasse 11/5
1100 Vienna, Austria

Belgium

Brussels
Hubbard Dianetics Foundation
45A, rue de l'Ecuyer
1000 Bruxelles, Belgium

Denmark

Aarhus
Hubbard Dianetics Foundation
Guldsmedegade 17, 2
8000 Aarhus C, Denmark

Copenhagen
Hubbard Dianetics Foundation
Store Kongensgade 55
1264 Copenhagen K, Denmark

Hubbard Dianetics Foundation
Vesterbrogade 66
1620 Copenhagen V, Denmark

France

Angers
Centre de Dianétique Hubbard
10–12, rue Max Richard
49000 Angers, France

Clermont-Ferrand
Centre de Dianétique Hubbard
1, rue des Ballainvilliers
63000 Clermont-Ferrand, France

Lyon
Centre de Dianétique Hubbard
3, place des Capucins
69001 Lyon, France

Paris
Centre de Dianétique Hubbard
65, rue de Dunkerque
75009 Paris, France

Centre de Dianétique Hubbard
Celebrity Centre Paris
69, rue Legendre
75017 Paris, France

St. Etienne
Centre de Dianétique Hubbard
24, rue Marengo
42000 St. Etienne, France

Germany

Berlin
Hubbard Dianetics Foundation
Sponholzstrasse 51/52
1000 Berlin 41, Germany

Düsseldorf
Hubbard Dianetics Foundation
Friedrichstrasse 28
4000 Düsseldorf, Germany

Hubbard Dianetics Foundation
Celebrity Centre Düsseldorf
Grupellostr. 28
4000 Düsseldorf, Germany

Frankfurt
Hubbard Dianetics Foundation
Darmstädter Landstrasse 213
6000 Frankfurt 70, Germany

Hamburg
Hubbard Dianetics Foundation
Steindamm 63
2000 Hamburg 1, Germany

Hubbard Dianetics Foundation
Celebrity Centre Hamburg
Mönckebergstrasse 5/IV
2000 Hamburg 1, Germany

Hanover
Hubbard Dianetics Foundation
Hubertusstrasse 2
3000 Hanover 1, Germany

München
Hubbard Dianetics Foundation
Beichstrasse 12
D-8000 München 40, Germany

Stuttgart
Hubbard Dianetics Foundation
Hirschstrasse 27
7000 Stuttgart 1, Germany

Israel

Tel Aviv
Hubbard Dianetics Foundation
7 Salomon Street
Tel Aviv 66023, Israel

Italy

Brescia
Hubbard Dianetics Foundation
Dei Tre Laghi
Via Fratelli Bronzetti, 20
25125 Brescia, Italy

Catania
Hubbard Dianetics Foundation
Via Giuseppe Garibaldi, 9
95121 Catania, Italy

Milano
Hubbard Dianetics Foundation
Via Abetone, 10
20137 Milano, Italy

Monza
Hubbard Dianetics Foundation
Via Cavour, 5
20052 Monza, Italy

Novara
Hubbard Dianetics Foundation
Corso Cavallotti, 7
28100 Novara, Italy

Nuoro
Hubbard Dianetics Foundation
Via G. Deledda, 43
08100 Nuoro, Italy

Padova
Hubbard Dianetics Foundation
Via Mameli, 1/5
35131 Padova, Italy

Pordenone
Hubbard Dianetics Foundation
Via Montereale, 10/C
33170 Pordenone, Italy

Roma
Hubbard Dianetics Foundation
Via di San Vito, 11
00185 Roma, Italy

Turino
Hubbard Dianetics Foundation
Via Guarini, 4
10121 Torino, Italy

Verona
Hubbard Dianetics Foundation
Vicolo Chiodo, 4/A
37121 Verona, Italy

Netherlands

Amsterdam
Hubbard Dianetics Foundation
Nieuwe Zijds Voorburgwal 271
1012 RL Amsterdam, Netherlands

Norway

Oslo
Hubbard Dianetics Foundation
Storgata 9
0155 Oslo 1, Norway

Portugal

Lisbon
Instituto de Dianética
Rua Actor Taborda 39–4°
1000 Lisboa, Portugal

Spain

Barcelona
Dianética
Calle Pau Claris 85, Principal 1ª
08010 Barcelona, Spain

Madrid
Asociación Civil de Dianética
Montera 20, Piso 1° DCHA
28013 Madrid, Spain

Sweden

Göteborg
Hubbard Dianetics Foundation
Odinsgatan 8
411 03 Göteborg, Sweden

Malmö
Hubbard Dianetics Foundation
Simrishamnsgatan 10
21423 Malmö, Sweden

Stockholm
Hubbard Dianetics Foundation
St. Eriksgatan 56
11234 Stockholm, Sweden

Switzerland

Basel
Hubbard Dianetics Foundation
Herrengrabenweg 56
4054 Basel, Switzerland

Bern
Hubbard Dianetics Foundation
Schulhausgasse 12
3113 Rubigen
Bern, Switzerland

Genève
Centre de Dianétique Hubbard
9 Route de Saint-Julien
1227 Carouge
Genève, Switzerland

Lausanne
Centre de Dianétique Hubbard
10, rue de la Madeleine
1003 Lausanne, Switzerland

Zürich
Hubbard Dianetics Foundation
Badenerstrasse 294
CH-8004 Zürich, Switzerland

Australia

Adelaide
Hubbard Dianetics Foundation
24 Waymouth Street
Adelaide, South Australia 5000
Australia

Brisbane
Hubbard Dianetics Foundation
2nd Floor, 106 Edward Street
Brisbane, Queensland 4000
Australia

Canberra
Hubbard Dianetics Foundation
Suite 16, 108 Bunda Street
Civic Canberra
A.C.T. 2601, Australia

Melbourne
Hubbard Dianetics Foundation
44 Russell Street
Melbourne, Victoria 3000
Australia

Perth
Hubbard Dianetics Foundation
39–41 King Street
Perth, Western Australia 6000
Australia

Sydney
Hubbard Dianetics Foundation
201 Castlereagh Street
Sydney, New South Wales 2000
Australia

Japan

Tokyo
Hubbard Dianetics Foundation
101 Toyomi Nishi Gotanda Heights
2-13-5 Nishi Gotanda
Shinagawa-ku
Tokyo, Japan 141

New Zealand

Auckland
Hubbard Dianetics Foundation
32 Lorne Street
Auckland 1, New Zealand

Africa

Bulawayo
Hubbard Dianetics Foundation
74 Abercorn Street
Bulawayo, Zimbabwe

Cape Town
Hubbard Dianetics Foundation
13 Hout Street
Cape Town 8001, South Africa

Durban
Hubbard Dianetics Foundation
57 College Lane
Durban 4001, South Africa

Harare
Hubbard Dianetics Foundation
First Floor, State Lottery Building
PO Box 3524
Corner Speke Avenue And Julius
  Nyerere Way
Harare, Zimbabwe

Johannesburg
Hubbard Dianetics Foundation
Security Building, 2nd Floor
95 Commissioner Street
Johannesburg 2001, South Africa

Hubbard Dianetics Foundation
101 Huntford Building
40 Hunter Street
Corner Hunter and Fortesque Roads
Yeoville 2198
Johannesburg, South Africa

Port Elizabeth
Hubbard Dianetics Foundation
2 St. Christopher
27 Westbourne Road Central
Port Elizabeth 6001, South Africa

Pretoria
Hubbard Dianetics Foundation
1st Floor City Centre
272 Pretorius Street
Pretoria 0002, South Africa

Colombia

Bogotá
Centro Cultural de Dianética
Carrera 19 No. 39–55
Apartado Aéreo 92419
Bogotá, D.E. Colombia

Mexico

Guadalajara
Organización Cultural Dianética de
  Guadalajara, A.C.
Av. López Mateos Nte.
329 Sector Hidalgo
Guadalajara, Jalisco, México

Mexico City
Asociación Cultural Dianética, A.C.
Hermes No. 46
Colonia Crédito Constructor
C.P. 03940 México 19, D.F.

Instituto de Filosofía Aplicada, A.C.
Durango #105
Colonia Roma
C.P. 06700 México, D.F.

Instituto de Filosofía Aplicada, A.C.
Plaza Río de Janeiro No. 52
Colonia Roma
C.P. 06700 México, D.F.

Instituto Tecnológico de
  Dianética, A.C.
Londres 38, 5TO piso
Colonia Juárez
C.P. 06600 México, D.F.

Organización, Desarrollo y
  Dianética, A.C.
Providencia 1000
Colonia Del Valle
C.P. 03100 México, D.F.

Centro de Dianética Polanco
Insurgentes Sur 536, 1er piso
  Esq. Nogales
Colonia Roma Sur
C.P. 06700 México, D.F.

Venezuela

Valencia
Asociación Cultural Dianética de
  Venezuela, A.C.
Ave. 101 No. 150–23
Urbanización La Alegría
Apartado Postal 833
Valencia, Venezuela

To obtain any books or cassettes by L. Ron Hubbard which are not available at your local organization, contact any of the following publishers:

Bridge Publications, Inc.
4751 Fountain Avenue
Los Angeles, California 90029

Continental Publications Liaison Office
696 Yonge Street
Toronto, Ontario, Canada M4Y 2A7

NEW ERA Publications
  International ApS
Store Kongensgade 55
1264 Copenhagen K, Denmark

ERA DINÁMICA EDITORES,
  S.A. de C.V.
Nicolás San Juan No. 208
Colonia Del Valle
C.P. 03020 México, D.F.

NEW ERA Publications, Ltd.
78 Holmethorpe Avenue
Redhill, Surrey
England RH1 2NL

N.E. Publications Australia Pty. Ltd.
2 Verona Street
Paddington, New South Wales 2021
Australia

Continental Publications Pty. Ltd.
P.O. Box 27080
Benrose 2011
South Africa

NEW ERA Publications Italia Srl
Via L. G. Columella, 12
20128 Milano, Italy

NEW ERA Publications GmbH
Otto-Hahn-Strasse 25
6072 Dreieich 1, Germany

NEW ERA Publications France
111, Boulevard de Magenta
75010 Paris, France

New Era Publications España, S.A.
C/De la Paz, 4/1° DCHA
28012 Madrid, Spain

NEW ERA Publications Japan, Inc.
5-4-5-803 Nishi Gotanda
Shinagawa-ku
Tokyo, Japan 141